Praise for **THE LITTLE BOO**

"Hugh Prather has distilled a treasure trove of practical, spiritual wisdom in his *Little Book of Letting Go*. His gentle exercises and wonderful insights help deliver us into the precious present, alive and grateful for the gift of life."

—**Joan Borysenko,** Ph.D., author of *Minding the Body, Mending the Mind* and *A Woman's Journey to God*

"At last a book that not only counsels us to "let go" but that tells us exactly how to do it. . . . Here's a book that can make a real difference in our daily lives, not just in our heads."

—**Hal Zina Bennett,** author of *Write from the Heart*

"Practical while being humorous, this book addresses the most common of human struggles while offering ways to lift the soul to all it is capable of."

—**Lee Jampolsky,** Ph.D., psychologist and author of *Healing the Addictive Mind* and *Smile for No Good Reason*

Praise for **SPIRITUAL NOTES TO MYSELF**

"*Notes to Myself* lit a path within. *Spiritual Notes to Myself* is a gentle guide to walking the path daily. It is filled with wisdom and joy."

—**Robert Johnson,** author of *He* and *She*

"We all need to converse with spirit. It is the only true guide we have. Read and then start taking notes."

—**Bernie Siegel, M.D.,** author of *Love, Medicine and Miracles*

LOVE *and* COURAGE

HUGH PRATHER

LOVE *and* COURAGE

CONARI PRESS
Berkeley, California

Conari Press books are distributed by Publishers Group West.
Cover Photography: ©Masao Ota /Photonica
Cover Design: Lisa Buckley
Book Design: Claudia Smelser

LIBRARY OF CONGRESS CATALOGING-IN-PUBLICATION DATA
Prather, Hugh.
   Love and courage / Hugh Prather.
    p. cm.
   ISBN 1-57324-724-3
   1. Conduct of life. 2. Interpersonal relations.   I. Title.
   BF637.C5 P67 2001
   177-DC21   2001002142

Printed in Canada.
01 02 03 TRANSCONTINENTAL 10 9 8 7 6 5 4 3 2 1

To Gayle

INTRODUCTION

The book you are reading is an extensively rewritten and augmented edition of *Notes on Love and Courage,* originally published in 1977. My wife Gayle and I worked on it line by line, and we hope you are as happy with the results as we are.

In one sense this book is about the old values—unselfishness, loyalty, honesty, forgiveness, courage—qualities that traditionally have been thought of as the elements of good character. This focus is somewhat surprising, because much of my "formal" writing during the period before I put the original book together expressed a deeply felt cynicism. Yet when I went back to see what I had been writing in my diary, I found I had been reclaiming much of what I had discarded when I was younger. At the same time that I had been turning things upside down, another part of my mind had been putting them right side up.

When I was growing up I was taught that to do good was not enough; we must *be* good. And I was told that if we are good, that is, if to the best of our ability we are gentle, honest, patient, forgiving, we would reach the highest state possible. The assumption—that goodness could be sought—was not questioned. If we wanted to be more loving, and if we practiced, if we labored, if we made love the focus of our lives, we would, with certainty, become more loving. Insofar as I am able to judge my inner state at that time, I did become a better person. I was more solicitous of other people's happiness, more generous, more willing to give up time. I saw more of the beauty in other people and in the world. And I believe this happened largely because I worked at it.

When I entered business, I was encouraged to put my boyhood ideals to use. I was told that they were practical. Sincerity was convincing, a pleasant disposition was good public relations, to be nonjudgmental (to think positively) was a powerful tool that could transform one's salesmanship from impotence to dynamism. As a result the time came when even the mention of words such as *cheerfulness, unselfishness, humility, courtesy,* and *goodness* became sickening to me. I not only stopped believing in their value, I stopped believing in their possibility. Cheerfulness was phony, unselfishness was self-deceptive, humility was a weakness, courtesy was a form, and there was no such thing as absolute good.

Prejudice is blind even when it is prejudice against words. It is significant that so many religious teachers and prophets spent so much of their time simply urging people to be good, urging them to turn from that which destroys to that which heals. Were these people wasting their time trying to be good? If it's true that humans cannot improve through their own efforts, then they were wasting their time; for what is gained by firing a person's will if some predetermining principle ordains his or her progress? Or if human-kind's deepest urges are not positive, they were wasting their time. Any influence they had would eventually be undone. Or if there is no goodness, if it doesn't exist even as a potential, they were wasting their time. They were merely pointing at a myth.

Goodness as form—as a hypocritical, unfelt duty—is not goodness. Goodness as a sentence, or as words spoken from a dais, or as essays in an embossed volume, or as rules that can be taught, or as the unstated sanctions of a group, is not goodness. But there *is* goodness. Every fiber in us knows the worth of our lives. Not that we can't be bullied or deceived, not that we don't have complexes and unreasonable doubts, not that we haven't been ill treated—we have in fact been damaged. But we know that stillness abides in the heart and light comes forth from the soul.

Hugh Prather
February 14, 2001
Tucson, Arizona

LOVE *and* COURAGE

Are there any wholly useless encounters? I know
this: There are no insignificant people. There is no
one who isn't supposed to be here.

We need other people, not in order to stay alive, but to be fully human: to be affectionate, funny, playful, generous. How genuine is my capacity for love if there is no one for me to love, to laugh with, to treat tenderly, to be trusted by? I can love an idea or a vision, but I can't throw my arms around it. Unless there is someone to whom I can give my gifts, in whose hands I can entrust my dreams, who will forgive me my deformities, my aberrations, to whom I can speak the unspeakable, then I am not human. I am a thing, a gadget that performs but has no music.

We talked again last night. What he doesn't seem to
realize is that if he isn't loyal to someone, if there
isn't someone his guts will simply not allow him to
manipulate, then his life is going to be a succession
of deceits. His treacheries are so reasonable that he
thinks any understanding friend would forgive him.
But he will not be forgiven. Time and again he will
be abandoned. Loyalty is not reasonable. It is the
easiest sentiment of all to argue against. If we have
a friend, we sometimes act against our own best
interests. A time may come when we appear self-
destructive because we have this friend and there is
something we must do to help him. There are worse
things than losing time, losing money, losing
position, even than losing life; and when we love
someone we sense that. But what words could I use
that would reach inside him and trigger loyalty?
I couldn't explain why anyone would *want* to be
loyal, when he knows that he has the alternative
of acting rationally and living an orderly life.

Is your first responsibility to yourself? This question is misleading; that is, it misleads the person who takes it to heart. It's like asking, Must you shift your weight in order to walk? Of course you must, but those who concentrate first on shifting their weight will not walk well.

There are people whose feelings and well-being are
within our influence. We can never escape this fact.
The oneness that Gayle and I have worked to achieve
is now a swinging door. It not only means that when
I choose peace for myself, I choose peace for her, but
when I choose misery, that too becomes my
shrouded gift.

Individual growth can't take precedence over
relationships; it can't because it ceases to be growth
in the attempt.

8   "Love thy neighbor as thyself" does not imply, as I have heard stated so often, that one must first love oneself. It implies nothing more complicated than the fact that anything less than love is not love. Love does not exclude; it embraces. If we don't love someone outside ourselves, then very simply, we do not love ourselves.

Is love *in* me, or is it something apart from me that

works *through* me? I can reason either way, but I can't deny how it feels: It feels as if there are times when I am more myself than at others. When I love spontaneously, when it simply comes out and there is no pretext or calculation, I don't feel either like a container of some precious but foreign spirit or like a vehicle for a thing outside of me. I feel: That which loves is me. And when the impulse is to hurt and I follow that, I feel like a betrayer, and the *I* has gone out of me.

To separate out my relationship to myself and set it aside for more luxuriant attention may be pleasurable; it may even be useful, but like any surgery it becomes more dangerous the longer it lasts. I am immobilized and temporarily severed from the other half of life. Ultimately my character is defined by the quality of my sensitivity to other people. I exist in equilibrium. I am here to the degree I am there.

Today I acknowledge that I am not in a position to
judge what mistakes anyone is making or what
lessons anyone needs to learn. I don't know how far
someone has come or when that person will have a
breakthrough, I simply don't know what other
people should be doing. But when I think I do know,
I clearly am not doing
what I should be doing,
which is taking respon-
sibility for my own life.

I can't be found in myself; I discover myself in others. That much is clear. And I suspect that I also love and care for myself in others. It is only in helping someone else to awake that I awake. That's because to be awake is to be united, to be one. And to be asleep is to have a mind that is still divided into a world of warring figures. This simple pattern keeps recurring. A friend tells me of a problem or some misery in his or her life. I listen, or together we talk it out. Later I remember that I had been depressed or not feeling well before we met. The ailment is not only forgotten but discarded.

I spent the day being an heir. I had decided that no matter what else I did I would try to stay conscious of everything agreeable sent my way. Much has been written about the benefits of giving; I wanted to see what it would feel like to be a devoted receiver. It was pleasant. At times I felt like a person of great beauty. There was a flood of gifts from the New Mexico desert: stormclouds, birds, light on the mountains, and one rather gaily colored, though unassertive, winged something that walked in front of my cereal bowl. I wasn't surprised by most of that. What I hadn't expected was how much people in general appeared to be offering, especially people I didn't know. There is a natural outpouring from the human nature, more deliberate and sustained than I had noticed before. It comes in the form of gestures and looks and a certain endeavor in the voice, as well as outright good humor and helpfulness. It's an attitude that is often instinctive when one person is in the presence of another, and it is recognizably apart from the usual posturing. I am reminded of how some animals always stay close enough that at any time they can brush against each other.

I have a friend who is a good listener. If I tell her about some difficulty I'm having, I never get the feeling she is doing little more than waiting to say something supportive. Her primary concern is not to put on a show of being a good listener, but rather it's as though my problem has become her problem in all respects. She is intensely loyal, yet she doesn't automatically criticize the person I may be blaming. She has an instinct for knowing how much I love that person, and if I do she speaks gently because she is for me; by that I mean she wants for me what I want at the deepest level, and she knows when my anger is superficial. However, if the person is not significant to my life, her criticism so devours the individual that by the time she is through I can laugh at my foolishness. It is also my undeserved good fortune that this friend is my wife.

After he told me that his
younger brother had been
knifed and his eyes seemed
to be pleading with me to
do something to comfort
him, I spent fifteen or
twenty minutes giving him
the thoughts that had
helped me at times when I

had suffered. Then he said, "If my brother dies I will
die at the same moment. That's how close we are." I
felt foolish for having tried to solve things. There is a
kind of pain that is far beyond words, and I was too
busy being conscientious to notice it. He simply
needed someone to be with.

This day has been magical. I have been with three friends, one at a time, and I have learned that friends can transform you. The first held me up so I could see. I was able to distinguish the points where things touch, and where they divide, the essential forms coming at me from the future, new elements and consummations, and the old principles that must not be neglected. I could name them all. They spilled from my mouth. He was delighted with my concepts. He didn't seem to realize that he was the one who had given me the vision. My second friend made me gentle and earnest. She needed to talk, and so we talked for a long time. She thanked me for my concern as I was leaving, but she wouldn't have recognized me if I had been any other way. The third friend turned me into a clown, a jester, a creator of quips. I hadn't known my life was filled with so much absurdity. He laughed and laughed because he had made me so funny. My friends don't know what they have done today. It's nothing to them; they do it so often. I expect I must also cause a change in them. And so we——each a separate we——exist only in each other's presence. That is something precious, not to be walked away from easily, and something that has to be included in any definition of self-sufficiency.

Today at lunch Joe told me that he and Ann had decided to get married in three weeks. "That makes the engagement as long as the courtship." I found myself liking the absurd symmetry of that as much as Joe did. But what he said next worried me: "I've never met anyone quite like her; she has everything I could possibly want." He was filling in all the blanks. I have seen so many marriages and even friendships end when the inevitable realization comes that something was left out of the other person. Sometimes nothing more tangible can be cited than the vague feeling that "something was missing." Usually it can be pinpointed: "She wouldn't go bowling," or "He was humorless, totally humorless." Darleen once said to me, "Jim and I never talk books. If I want to talk books I visit Aunt May. Aunt May reads." So simple. It takes five to ten people to make up the one got-it-all friend we are looking for.

Something within me knows that most of what I am will die without people, and it doesn't behave itself . So I eventually surrender my seclusion and walk out the door. However, when the mind is given a problem to solve, its tendency is to select and fixate. That works well in a shoe store. But if I allow myself to become convinced that simply because a person is there, obvious and convenient, I am therefore in need of him or her, that if I don't make it with this individual I will be friendless, I not only create the likelihood that I will be disappointed, I also scare off the very person whose companionship I am seeking.

No one wants to be the only available source.

The window is not the view; the window allows the view.

All these people passing by. Every year another ocean of faces I will never see again. By using my eyes I can connect with a few, but only a few. And even that is often misunderstood. In a lifetime I will lay eyes on thousands of human beings— across rooms, on the street, inside buildings. What will come of it? Nothing. Absolutely nothing. Unless I change my attitude, they will remain a part of the dull background.

As I was walking back from Gary's office, I was remembering something funny he said. Several people passed me before I realized that most of them had smiled when they saw my face. This shows me a possibility of some general yet satisfying kind of stranger-to-stranger communication. I'm sure it's not to be found in rehearsed greetings or a prescribed sweetness of expression. It's probably a component of those mental states such as humor, love, and happiness, which, without trying, already include the people we meet.

However fatuously arrived at, even if it's that we
look into each other's eyes as we pass in the aisle of a store, something is formed by this crossing of two lives. For a moment a new mixture has been made. No matter how quickly done, I hand something over, whether at home with Gayle or on the street. Life's burning question is, What do we leave in our wake? It isn't grandeur and glory that give a life its eternal mark, but the love or lovelessness of these minuscule encounters that mount up day by day. Coming home today I was in a five o'clock line of cars driving down Paseo de Peralta. There was a little boy sitting on an adobe wall who was having the time of his life waving at each driver who went by. I didn't see one person who could refuse him.

I tried an experiment today. I walked around the plaza holding the thought that I had returned home but my appearance was so radically changed no one could recognize me. All these people used to be very good friends of mine, and I was amused and delighted to see them again and to discover how well they were doing. As I walked I maintained this attitude, but I didn't try to force eye contact. What I discovered was that there was one group, more than half, who were oblivious of me, but there was another group who nodded or smiled, and I had a peculiar feeling that they were in on the secret—but that the secret was not what I had thought. It wasn't that I was playing a game, but that we indeed were not strangers, that in some tangible sense our relationship had existed before that moment. Oneness is experienced as familiarity. We sense the familiar in those around us. And if it is familiar, it must have always been there.

Love sees things as they are. We feel understood by the people who like us, misunderstood by the people who don't—and those feelings are probably realistic.

We alone place limits on how many ways we can love.

Except briefly in elementary school I had never
played football, but in my senior year of high school
I decided to try out for the team. I liked the new
coach and I wanted to confront my fear of contact
sports, which I knew at times could be almost
incapacitating. It quickly became clear that the
coach had a much higher opinion of my abilities
than I did, and under his daily urgings I began to
transform in a way that seemed miraculous to me. I
not only made the first team but lettered. He had
seen what I was capable of and would accept nothing
less from me. When I went to college, the coach
there was indifferent. My fear returned and I
eventually stopped playing altogether. I had
experienced the power of being respected but not yet
the power of respecting myself.

There must be another way to go through life besides being pulled through it kicking and screaming.

Learning to accept yourself is the beginning of change. Learning to accept others is the beginning of wholeness. Love expands. It not only sees more and enfolds more, it causes its object to bloom.

When my self-esteem is a veneer, that is, when it stands on superficialities such as body, dress, glibness, and reputation, I am less sensitive to other people as people, as living, laughing, hurting human beings. I stop seeing people directly and only watch others for their reactions to me.

Our mistakes are merely instances in which we have limited our options.

Sometimes I wonder if my standard of loyalty to myself is as high as it is to my friends. I am capable of selling myself out just to make points. Where are the decency and fairness for all when I present myself with anything less than integrity? I downgrade myself in order to please, but of course it never pleases. It's not realistic to expect someone to feel more respect for me than I display for myself. Yet, paradoxically, I respect myself by respecting others. The key to confidence is not to marshal my strength and bolster my self-image. It is to think and act so as not to be preoccupied with myself.

30   When individuals respect themselves, it can be seen
in their posture, their voice, the integrity of their
opinions. But it can't be strategy. And it has nothing
to do with formality and restraint, because if we love
ourselves we can also abandon ourselves: we can
throw ourselves on the wind of love and know that
we will soar.

It's pure pleasure to be around Jim and his little boy.
No one could miss seeing how much they love each
other. Even their most petulant arguments are
touched with gentleness. Love isn't a war I'm
engaged in. If I truly like someone, my affection will
be recognized. When Gayle is on the phone it's clear
from her laugh and tone of voice how much she
likes the person at the other end. In attempting to
convince others that they are liked more than they
are, we often use an assiduous pressure. Love has no
need to show itself off. It can be seen in position.
Every muscle, every gesture, betrays it. Fill your
heart with love, and its expression will take care of
itself.

Love is uncovered; it is carefully disrobed, like folding back petals. It isn't a medal of sainthood.

As soon as they marry, many people get funny ideas about "rights." There is little hope for a marriage in which the overbalancing effort is to get the other person to behave. The person I want to live my life with is the person to whom I can give the greatest opportunity to do with her life what she wants.

A couple, who for the past nine years have had an almost ideal relationship, got married this Christmas. It lasted three weeks. It's not uncommon for a rancorous marriage to end in divorce and for the people to then live together quite harmoniously. In either case, the difference is the extent to which the two are willing to accept each other as they are.

34   Marriage isn't mutual ownership. It must be an act of trust in each other's good sense and good intentions. If a marriage is an expression of respect, then it adds grace to love and can soften the momentary selfishness that may cause a couple to let slip a friendship they have been building for years.

As of July, Gayle and I will have been married thirty-
six years. That means ours will be the longest
continuous relationship I have had. Before we got
married I couldn't have guessed that this simple
accumulation of years, taken by itself, would affect
the quality of my life. It has given it an added bit of
dignity: someone I admire has wanted to spend
thirty-six years of her life with me.

For many years my opinion of marriage was that it tends to be obstructive of growth, that it is a set of externally imposed restraints that often discourage the individual from leaving a relationship that is depleted. My assumption was that no relationship is eternal, that each has its own natural progression and span, and that the aware person can know the time to stay and the time to leave—why then enter into an agreement based only on the ideal of staying? I looked at long-term marriages with suspicion. After all, how much change could ten or twenty years with the same person allow? And when there is little variation, little stimulation, people are predisposed to remain as they are. Now my experience has shown me an alternative, and like

many other things that work, it doesn't argue well.
I am quite certain that Gayle and I would not be
together now if we had not consented to, or had not
constructed for ourselves, some type of deterrence
to leaving. By getting married, we agreed to try for
something lasting; we agreed to rules that would
make parting unpleasant; we pledged love, support,
and equal sharing of all that we had; and we declared
this publicly so that if we failed it would be known.
This was not a reasonable thing to do. I remember
the night we drove to Oklahoma so that we could
get married in two hours. I kept saying to myself,
"I'm making a big mistake." Thirty-six years later, I
know that my intuition allowed for a possibility that
my reason would have precluded.

Whenever I take a long run, I go through one or two periods when my body feels like shutting down. If I were to follow its lead I would slow to a walk. Had this consistently been my response when I first began cross-country running, I would never have become conditioned to last long enough to explore the badlands and discover old cave dwellings. I have seen this pattern before. There have been other times when I reached a physical, creative, or spiritual plateau and then overrode what felt like a natural restraint. The results were that I broke into what was for me a new territory (with its own new boundaries). There is something to be said for going through resistance. Sometimes we have to break with habit and do what feels unnatural.

The closest thing to a long-term marriage that I
have experienced was the mandatory change of
roommates we had each ninety days at boarding
school. Everything would look the same—the
room, the schedule—except suddenly you were
living with a stranger. Over the years, that happens
with remarkable frequency in marriage. You
consider your relationship perfectly fine as it is, but
all at once this person, whom you thought you had
long since figured out, begins to transform. And you
know that if you want to stay married, you will have
to become more flexible. The type of growth
demanded is somewhat unusual, for even though
you can see merit in the changes, you would be
content to stay as you are, and so you find yourself
changing out of love for someone else. That is often
more difficult, but also more satisfying, than
essentially self-interested, self-congratulatory
improvement.

Love, the magician, knows this little trick whereby
two people walk in different directions yet always
remain side by side.

Very seldom do we give up on ourselves. We
continue to have hope because we know we have the
potential for change. We try again—not just to exist,
but to bring about those changes in ourselves that
will make our lives worth living. Yet people are very
quick to give up on friends—and especially on their
partners—to declare them hopeless, and either to
walk away or do nothing more than resign
themselves to a bad situation. It is possible for people
to be "open and honest" with their partners without
attacking them. But that is seldom how openness
and honesty are practiced. If "honoring our feelings"
is the goal, it's also possible to beat pillows, scream
into the wind, go for a run, or release our bodily
tensions in some other harmless way, and still
respect ourselves. It is curious that we think that in
order to be "true to ourselves," we must hurt
someone else.

I am comfortable around my friend. For reasons not always clear to me, she loves me. She has seen me blunder; she is aware of my annoying self-indulgences, my private habits. All the things I once thought no one could know about me and still love me, she knows. In her presence I have very little to guard against, because she distills me from my words. We have been together a long time, and now some grace within her can see me even when her eyes are open.

the quiet thoughts
of two people a long time in love
touch lightly
like birds nesting in each other's warmth
you will know them by their laughter
but to each other
they speak mostly through their silence
if they find themselves apart
they may dream of sitting undisturbed
in each other's presence
of wrapping themselves warmly in each
    other's ease

The way two people make love is not the weather vane of their relationship. I have known couples who had great sex who broke up, and I have known couples who had no sex and are still happily together.

Getting their dates to bed can become some individuals' mission. They may succeed with the body, but in the process they waste the soul. They cannot feel that exchange of spirits after which one walks away having gathered life. They in fact die a little more each time they attempt to crucify love.

Intercourse in which the other person is left out is masturbation, and anyone who has been used in that way knows what it feels like to be a device.

People who fold their clothes neatly and settle down to business fail to notice that sex is not a solemn duty. Healthy sex is a form of mutual laughter— both people get the joke.

46   A few months after I dropped out of college, I came back on campus to visit an English professor from whom I had taken two courses. Although my wording was somewhat oblique, I succeeded in informing her that I found her attractive and that I thought it would be a good idea if we made love. Teaching me one final lesson, she got out her appointment book and said, "What about a week from Wednesday after my three o'clock class?"

The erotic receives its force not just from flesh and
the sheer weight of bodies, but from the silver of
subtleties: acts begun and not completed, silences
created, words withheld, rhythm building upon
rhythm, startling intrusions, tenderness, and
overwhelming waves of peace. For such magic one
must first remove one's head. At times, nonverbal
communication can be virtually a thing Divine. In
just a glance, a reality almost blissful in its intimacy
can pass between strangers. Something from that
other world where everything is known must live
inside the eyes.

Each individual we encounter appears to hold a lost piece of us. It joins with us the instant it is recognized. But only love can see it.

Love cannot be restrained. Nor can judgment be
focused and circumscribed. If I am truly accepting of
one person, then I become more accepting of all
people. Yet if I judge one person, soon I am judging
everyone.

To want something from another is to utterly
misunderstand their role in our happiness. Other
people are our opportunity to extend what we *are*.

Most people assume that in a loving relationship individuals agree with each other. Many people, for example, become scared or shaken when their partner disagrees with them. Then they compound the mistake by trying to change their partner's mind. Yet on a personality level, two people are different in all respects and cannot be made identical in any way. There are no well-matched couples. Friendship is seeing differences, accepting differences, yet continuing to love and be happy.

It is good and natural to doubt ourselves. Those who do not doubt can easily mislead themselves. When properly used, doubt keeps me humble, balanced, and open to learning from others. Thinking I am wise is an absolute block to wisdom.

Accepting responsibility does not mean accepting blame.

If I actively look for differences and accept each one I see, I notice that my basic bond with a person is not threatened or even touched by our differences. Looked at this way, other people's differences become interesting and entertaining. They add to, rather than subtract from, the richness of the relationship. Interestingly, comfort with ourselves, not war, is the agent for change. And accepting another's personality is the starting point for an improved friendship.

How can reluctance to look at the precise ways I think and act destructively make me less destructive? Admitting that we are powerless can take two distinct forms. One says, "I am powerless over my inner demons," and gives into them. The other makes the same admission, and asks for help.

Actively and persistently searching out my mental mistakes does not make my mind more negative—because these are mistakes I was *already* making. Once I have seen it clearly, I can look past my shadow side to my gentler side. Now the place of sanity is not so easily lost, because I know exactly how I arrived there.

My own nonsense must be recognized as nonsense,
but once I recognize it, I can forget it. It will not
come back to bite me, because its only effects were
the ones I myself chose. This means I don't need to
look over my shoulder when I am happy. In every
life a little sunshine must fall. This is normal, so get
over it. I think that keeping my guard up means I
must keep my mind focused on my archives of
worries, as if the universe keeps score and when it
sees that I'm not receiving my quota of hardships, it
corrects the imbalance.

The introvert has no advantage over the extrovert. It works either way. As we grow to understand and accept ourselves, we become more tolerant of others. If we gain a new appreciation of someone else, that pulls with it our opinion of ourselves. I would never have guessed that seeing my limitations more clearly would make me more tolerant.

Human beings are too complex to be taken in
whole, to be seen in all their parts, to be assessed in a
moment. Even if it were possible, an instant later
their mood has changed; they have remembered
some act of kindness or humiliation, or a thing
unseen has poured into them, even as it has into the
eyes that judge them. The only way I can judge
another is to see him or her as one thing. If,
however, I take in all of a person's varied and
contradictory aspects, there is no story to tell, no
"type" to be classified, and any decision I have
already made about this person is seen as lacking and
arbitrary.

58   The notion that negative thoughts and feelings should be "honestly" expressed, or "vented," comes from the assumption that if you "get it out," it is no longer in. But ideas do not leave their source, and all criticism attacks the criticizer. When I allow my words to reflect my negative mood, the negativity becomes more deeply rooted and powerful, and I stir up the other person as well. Now the problem takes on a life of its own and is out of my control.

In order to point my finger in praise or
condemnation, in order to know some quality
whether it is sweet or sour, in order to recognize it,
that characteristic must in some way reside in me. It
isn't possible to be enlightened and know it. What
you hold yourself superior to is a part of you.

The character of a church, a business, or a government can be seen in its attitude toward its detractors.

Friends eventually forgive and come back together because people need people more than they need pride.

Most of us don't look at things, we look at aspects of things. Our interests are specific. We don't see people, we see clothes or bodies or mirrors of our performance, or we see our own projections of pettiness, bitterness, superiority, or weakness. And slowly we become what we disapprove of most. Thought directs the eyes, and eyes direct the soul.

One of the things I don't like about myself is my capacity for dismissing certain people. I did it again tonight. I was introduced to a man who instead of saying, "Hello," said, "Whassup?" and I thought, *Oh God another one of those.* On the spot I wrote him off. On what possible grounds can I judge someone that quickly? I know this is the same quality in me that on occasions makes me squirm with inferiority.

Perhaps there are some individuals I should back away from as soon as I meet them. However, there's a difference between dismissing a person because I am being controlled by some mindless, reflexive bias, and ridding my life of an individual whom I can see—because I am looking clearly—bears me no goodwill.

There are always people around who need the illusion of rising by putting someone else down. The interesting thing about this type of exchange is that the one who is getting worked over usually doesn't realize it. That happened tonight at Nat's slide show. Dewey was getting it good from a man I had never met, and everyone knew it except Dewey, who, with almost touching earnestness, kept setting himself up. There is a surprisingly widespread disbelief in malice. We don't like to think we can be readily disliked. Nevertheless, someone who has a general desire to make others feel ill at ease doesn't need good reason. In any group of people there is usually as much effort being directed at causing discomfort as there is straightforward goodwill. I am beginning to see that our egos are more powerful and destructive than I believed when I was idealistic simply to be idealistic.

After being with Langley, I have to scrub down my opinion of every friend he has ever met. I sit here listening to him analyze people I have known for years, and it's like being fed a kind of slow poison. I realize his criticisms are mostly accurate, but the effect is to magnify their failings and so disfigure them that by the time he is finished, my good opinion of them has lessened. I think I am probably betraying them by even listening; it clearly feels that way.

I'm fond of Langley. He is eloquently droll and consistently unboring. Yet I almost always come away not liking myself. Because of his wit I hesitate to connect him with this aftertaste, but I know other people who can affect me the opposite way: I leave them feeling I have been set in flight or handed something old of great value. I am naïve to think he could wish the best for me when he is so embittered toward everyone else. If being around a person of goodwill is empowering, then this generalized ill will could certainly cause me to feel diminished.

What can I learn from Langley? Perhaps that no one has a private state of mind. And although our dominant attitude will have its effect on others whether we want it to or not, if we pour that attitude into every word and act, the effect is all the greater. That means if my ego is boiling I should put the lid on it so it doesn't splatter on everyone else.

My mind is like every other mind—it is capable of almost any bizarre thought. I don't have to speak "honestly" about these thoughts. In fact, they are so random and contradictory that it would be impossible to voice them all without sounding like a babbling idiot. Instead, I must sink below the chatter into my quieter core.

Live as if everything you do will eventually be known. And treat others as if you can see the effects before you act.

In what order are souls ranked today? All morning I have been receiving calls: "What did so-and-so mean by that?"—"Why wasn't I invited?"—"What did she say?"—"I thought I was her best friend." I hope I have lost my tolerance for intrigue. It is a demeaning waste of time. Friendship can't result from brilliant footwork. Here you've plotted and sweated and schemed and now you're considered by everyone to be a person's best friend. Does that make the time you spend with that individual one bit more enjoyable?

A curious reciprocity runs through most aspects of human relationships. Canceled engagements and turned-down invitations are an example. If it isn't suitable for one, more often than not the change in plans works out best for the other. There is no obvious reason why this should be true, and my inclination is to react as if a change in plans is a mistake without waiting to see what effect the change will have.

We were having dinner. I asked Gene if that was his
friend John R. who just walked in. He said yes.
"Aren't you going to speak to him?" "No," he said. "I
never speak to anyone in public. All that happens is
you ask oily, nimble-footed questions about each
other's imaginary lives. And you know the most
you're going to get is a weather report. It tires me
out because I'm no good at social skills. I've told
everyone I'm nearsighted."

If we hold to the impossible ideal that a world of separate egos with separate agendas can be perfected, our efforts will be thwarted and our emotions will

deteriorate into cynicism. Hope must not be placed in a better world, but in a true heart and a gentle vision.

So often I worry about a decision before it has to be
made. When the time comes to decide, I will always
know more than I do now about both the situation
and my own feelings. And interestingly, one
recurring phenomenon is that the very information
needed to make the best choice often doesn't arrive
until it is time for a decision.

Honesty can be gentle—that's what so much of this popularized bluntness lacks, this everything-gut-level, this point-blank-on-all-occasions. It is humorless posturing, a mode of superiority, and it's exhausting to be around. I want to be honest out of respect. And if I must lie in order to spare someone senseless pain, then it is my responsibility to lie so well that it won't be given a second thought.

If we knew everything that was ever said about us,
and if at the same time we took every word at face
value, we would remain friends with no one. When
we are critical of a third person, often we are not
convinced; we say it for the effect it will have on the
people we are with—a form of confiding, a way of
uniting. Gossip is simply a universal human
language. And it can be a lot of fun—if it doesn't
include bitterness.

It's becoming clear to me that none of us fully knows what we are saying. In conversation we don't have the luxury of a rough draft. Just take a good look at individuals trying to talk: every time they open their mouths it's an experiment and a gamble, often a minor disaster. Our friends are the ones who don't hold this against us. Even if one had unlimited time to word each thought, there is no fact or feeling so obvious, so simple, that it would fit perfectly into a sentence.

It's not how much I've been mistreated in the past,
but my fear of acknowledging my contribution to
the effects in the present that keeps me stuck.

Sometimes a person's contribution to pain is no
more than holding onto a wound long after it could
have healed. No one need remain living proof of
another's guilt.

I hurt because I refuse to take responsibility. Pain
breaks down my resistance to awareness. If it's really
pain, and if I see it clearly, I can't deny the price I pay
for being a victim. Nothing I do makes it go away. It
grips me until I am ready to admit that what I hold
on to is what I have.

Pain can never be taken philosophically; otherwise it isn't pain. Our eyes have not been opened. The more humane we become, the more likely we are to suffer. Approachable means vulnerable, woundable. Not made hard by a history of abuse, but like old leather, made softer, more comfortable to be near. I can be inspired to grow, but more often I grow because my pride has been broken by certain unyielding realities. When I have once again been made aware of my fallibility, I become predisposed to learn.

There is a time to let things happen and a time to
make things happen. No one becomes permanently
comfortable. Life is not solved. Like a large
hibernating animal it turns on its belly and once
again we have to crawl out from under it. If we don't
move, we die.

If it is not given me to know the course of time, then the best I can do is to be attentive, to watch carefully what is happening, to feel out the direction, to sense what movement I can. It's like trying to work my way along a wall in the dark. It doesn't serve me to turn and rail against the wall; it may have been placed there for my protection.

One element of maturity is the realization that we don't get away with anything. Any advantage gained or convenience taken, any private procrastination or insincerity, no matter how subtle or quick in passing, is paid for. Not dramatically. Often not noticeably. But enough that we learn, eventually, it is not worth it. Progress is dirty business. We are taught the smell of the ego's reward as well as the fragrance of the heart.

If every problem must be worked through, if it's true I will not be saved by the bell, that death will not release me of a single necessity, then I want to stop, right now, putting off what I know must eventually be dealt with. Either we are throwing our emotional weight into the balance of fear and anger or we are adding to the world's measure of hope and kindness. This cannot be seen, of course, but it certainly can be felt.

We are born into a life. The life is waiting there. We
don't pick it, we step into it—parents, first born or
last, the part of the country, the part of the world,
our appearance, the efficiency of our brain. Then a
time comes when we realize that we also have
choices, and so we begin the task of building our
own life—an impossible task considering the
number of days we are given to complete it.
However, I don't think that's important; what is
important is to begin.

It was back in the '70s that Rusty pointed out a waitress who was taking orders at the next table. He said that four years ago she was married, had a fourteen-year-old daughter, and was the school system's consultant on dyslexia. It was summer. She and her husband were having a drink in a bar in Aransas Pass. Her husband went to the restroom, and while he was gone a man at the other end of the bar said, "Hi. Would you like to come with me to Mexico?" On the spot she walked out. She lived with the man for three years in Guatemala. Even uglier than the story was the reaction at our table. We all stared at the woman as if she were a heroine. Any person who can't feel the distress of a child waiting for a parent to return, or of a life mate abandoned on a whim, is for that moment an edifice without soul. A time comes when you need to clean house. No, you need to go even further, you need to burn the house down with yourself inside it. Then you must walk from the fire and say, I have no name.

Yes there are other considerations. There is no end to the considerations—the feelings of the parent who leaves, the possible consequences of staying, the hope for a better life. But a time can come when you have "loved" and "nurtured" yourself so much that there just isn't much of you left. And all you have is enough strength to act, just enough to put an end to it by turning away from your "best interests" and wading back into the mud of relationship. I can't help anyone by losing my soul. In fact, if it's beginning to destroy me, I can be confident it's not helping you.

There is something to be said for writing out my beliefs just so I can question them. There is something to be said for setting down the pattern of my life just so I can break with it.

Just because it's what you do best doesn't mean you have to do it.

I have finished reading several accounts of possession and I'm intrigued with one of the ramifications. The old personality leaves and a new personality takes over the old body. Now, if I were the new occupant and today I was moving into this person named Hugh, I would make a sign out of precious metal and hang it around his neck. It would say, "Under New Management." I would have nothing to lose; no tired, uninspired self-indulgences that must be maintained for God knows what reason; no habits— dressing habits, eating habits; no demeanor to preserve. I could forgive old enemies and revive old relationships because I would have no pride to protect. I could throw off any mannerism, take up any endeavor, study any subject, move anywhere— the world would be my playground, and I would be as free as a child to make new friends.

When I lose my sensitivity to those quiet seepages from the other side of reality, my world becomes stubborn and flat, and I notice a lack of balance in most of the activities I undertake. A few weeks ago I decided to look for more deliberate ways to attach myself to that other side, and I began to experiment with precognition. On any given day there are numerous opportunities to make a prediction: Someone is coming—what time will he or she arrive? The phone rings—who is it? I make a call— will the person be there? I started out by simply asking a question (for example, what team will win?). The results were no better than if I had guessed. Then I tried seeing the future incident, the way you might try to remember what the person who just left had been wearing. I had the least success with numbers (for example, exact scores), but when I tried picturing the people involved— for instance two of the contestants and their emotional states immediately after a match—and from that picture deducing who had won, I got good results. In trying to determine whether someone is home before I call, I picture the house and mentally go through each room. I usually get a firm impression of whether or not the house is empty. It is not altogether surprising that I can sense the mental states of specific people more clearly than I can the answers to abstract questions. The aspect of the future that I will experience most strongly (and which will therefore stand out most clearly) will be human and complex rather than numerical and precise.

Joe Osmond was once in a coma for two months. After he came out of it, he rested a few more days in the hospital and then resumed his life. "Nothing had changed," he said. We think the details of our lives are so important. But it's worth noting how much simply does not have to get done. It's a perverse aspect of human nature that when faced with a crisis or even increased stress, our tendency is to do *more,* and especially to do what does not need to be done *now.*

This afternoon I started telling two of my relatives about my experiences with precognition. They didn't want to hear about them. They told me that

parapsychology was the work of the devil. I've
encountered this attitude before. It always comes
from people with similar religious beliefs. They quote
the same biblical passages, which indicates that their
conclusions have been shared and not arrived at
individually. Why do most of us feel the need to
receive our attitudes from someone else? It's as if we
don't want our own minds. When Gayle and I first
moved here, we were told by several people that
piñon jays were obnoxious birds. I tried to see them
that way, but late in the summer I finally succumbed
to my own unsophisticated view that they were
hilariously preposterous. What interests me is that I
would attempt to react as I had been told. The
majority's opinion, especially if it's negative, is
assumed to be more intelligent. This may come in
part from the distrust we learn as children in the
accuracy of our own judgment. As adults I believe
there is not much pleasure in it, unless it's in the
feeling of community and in being right.

I have been working on the finish carpentry in the kitchen. Today was my first time to make and set drawers. I noticed that as I got about halfway through each new phase of the process, I was thinking to myself, "It's never as easy as it looks." Suddenly I didn't like my habitual way of looking at tasks, even if in this instance it was honest. So I decided to be phony and say over and over, "It's always easier than it looks." As soon as I began this, the work became less difficult. It was as if someone had injected me with a vial of knowledge on how to make drawers. However, I suspect the same results would have occurred if I had been an inveterate and self-deceiving positive thinker and suddenly admitted that the task before me was difficult. A task is not one thing. The trick is to allow each little aspect of a task to come to us in the present.

After dinner Oliver came by and sat next to Mr.
Mayer, who was across the room from me on the
couch. They introduced themselves, then I watched
that miracle that sometimes happens when two
people come together and at once their minds
synchronize. That has happened to me, and there
are times when I feel myself striving to bring it about
again, especially if I am talking to someone I have
just met. When it comes unforced, the phenomenon
is almost supernatural. As in some moments of love,
there is a feeling of each of us being totally contained
within the other. I begin surprising myself with what
I say. I state insights that an instant before I didn't
know I had. Were they always inside me, but now
this person is pulling them out? It feels more nearly
as if together we have formed a new mind which
until that moment did not exist.

There is this other reality about which a lot is written but very little is experienced. Even though it is unavoidable, we somehow manage. Perhaps only in retrospect do we see it plainly— so plainly that the vision itself does not allow us to proceed with life, but stands waiting for us behind every inconvenient corner. But then we lose it by formulating systems designed to transform human nature and revolutionize the world. Of course they never do. Because we are trying to use reality instead of be it. Concepts only box a corpse. Truth, which is whole, cannot be applied to personal perception, which is random, separate, and chaotic. When truth is stated, intelligent people dismiss it, then stop looking at even those small but persistent evidences within their own lives. They continue their conversations as if there were only a single dimension, as if everything grew out of the one flat piece of soil they stand on, as if they don't die, don't dream, don't wake up in the night sweating, don't reach for the phone knowing, don't feel their diseases melt from them in the presence of the one they love, don't sense their child calling to them, don't see their friends walk whole before them in their deaths.

There are moments when I sense that something else is going on, something I knew a long time ago, as though there were once a time when I knew what was behind all of this but now I have forgotten. Sometimes when I wake from a dream it seems I am almost remembering it, or I hear it in the respiration of the waves or see it in the stars when they're so heavy that's all you can look at; even during the instant of stillness when my car was skidding broadside off the road. Throughout my life I have kept returning to that same familiarity. The opposite of a nameless fear. At times I think I am looking down at myself, vaguely recalling that all this shouldn't be taken too seriously, an almost certain conviction that I am not that thing walking around down there.

The differing natures of day and night can't be explained by the absence of light alone. Something moves at night. There is a presence. The demons come out, but so do the Muses. Perhaps stars are there to remind us of the nearness of angels. At sunset the birds flock to the big cottonwood beside our house. They chatter, jump from limb to limb, then slowly settle in and grow quiet. In the morning, they don't precipitously bolt from the tree. First they return to their song. On the other hand, we, the intelligent species, try to race headlong into sleep and take no real time in the morning to collect ourselves and begin the day with a clear sense of who we are. Strange that this potentially meditative and restorative state before, during, and after sleep is not considered part of real life. It is never highlighted in biographies or magazine profiles. What we do with this time is not considered an accomplishment or failure worth mentioning.

It happened again this morning. I woke up and for a few seconds I didn't know who or where I was. It seems evident that a filtering or separating process takes place during sleep. My name, location, age, and gender were not present; my worldly identity had to re-enter my mind; I had to download my ego. I had been stripped of all the seemingly essential who-are-you, what-are-you answers. I didn't know what I had been doing or what I was going to do, and yet I had a clear sense of continuation, of being, of ongoing existence. I was not panicked; I did not feel newborn; I was familiar to myself. And for the moment that vivid and peaceful awareness was all I had, all I wanted. Whenever the state lasts more than a few seconds, I become anxious, but this fear

always accompanies the start of certain thoughts
such as, "I know this room but I don't know my
name." Many times I have awakened and a moment
later the first thing that gets my attention is a sense
of doom, sadness, or elation. Then the memory
follows that explains why I feel that way: the day
before my grandfather died, or I received a letter of
acceptance from a publisher, and the like. There is
an apparent order in which the previous contents re-
enter my mind. First the almost unconscious
thought, then the emotion, then the "reality" of my
situation. Even more fascinating is the pattern: first
the location, then the identity. I am here therefore I
am Hugh.

In just one night's dreaming the mind roams up and down the ages, wanders into other minds, and disregards the boundaries of future and past. I close my eyes and hear voices, but I am coming into the middle of something. A conversation is in progress. The participants are indifferent to my arrival. One of them is me. I was having this other conversation and didn't know it. Yet when I awake, I now think I am back in control.

The second day out of Santa Fe I woke up in the motel, but the dream I had been having didn't stop. Even though I was fully awake, it continued its progression sharp and undiminished for a period of seven or eight seconds. If I add this experience to the apparently random manner in which my mind steps into a dream, the conclusion I come to is that the dream world or the dreaming mind is ongoing. It is reached through sleep but is not activated by sleep. My present sense of it is that even at this moment it is acting out its commentary, its allegorical parody, of my relationship to myself and to a profusion of other lives. At any given instant during the day, I am probably causing new eddies of dream stories that, if I knew how, I could see as clearly as I see the tracks I leave behind in an arroyo.

There have been other nights like this one when I have awakened knowing that I have been fighting with something for hours. A terrible struggle with something. I am exhausted. I have won—I know that because I am here, but I know too that it will come again. My dreams, my nighttime battles, tell me unequivocally that I want to be good. I am trying, God knows I am trying, to wash off this slime of self-betrayal.

I wonder if all the attention I am giving my dreams is like standing on a ship and studying the wake to see what I need to do now, when all the while the hole that is sinking the ship is right beside me.

 I know of no more deadly state of mind than the one in which I become preoccupied with money and possessions. Every time I start comparing my house, clothes, car, and income against those of my friends, I feel my personality twisting into a deformity. There will always be those who are "better off" than I and those who are not, and no other fact could be more irrelevant to life's meaning. It isn't so much whether we have a little or a lot, it's how we *think* about money and possessions that can diminish us. Having too little can be a tragedy; it can even lead to death. Yet, strangely, having too much can be so preoccupying for some people that they never live.

I am continually underestimating my capacity for selfishness. I like to think of myself as generous, especially toward my friends, but I'll suddenly see new uses for some old possession I am about to give away, or in the middle of a favor—that I have offered to do—I begin resenting the time it's taking. I wish I weren't afraid. I wish I could loosen my grip and enjoy the very simple pleasure of giving.

I can't throw off the habits of a lifetime. To attempt

to do so is to lose ground. It's a question of which
way to look. In a marathon the person in second
place is usually the one who looks over his or her
shoulder. So long as I am battling my immaturity, I
am not allowing myself to grow up. Why become
engaged with sweeping my path of old footsteps,
when I can take new ones? When I choose the old
darkness, it's all still there, and I am again capable of
mistakes I thought I had long since put behind me.
The ego can't be perfected, but all of us are free to
choose the stillness of our heart.

Life is not just, even though our sense of justice is one part of life. Yet if we abandon our personal sense of right and wrong because it's not the standard by which reptiles and insects operate, we betray ourselves and so become an enemy to our own substance. The paradox is that although life is not righteous, we make peace with our life only through righteousness.

I can't determine what I should do by guessing how things will play out. I don't know how things will play out, but I do know what I believe, because belief is in the present. So the question becomes, "What do I believe is the simplest, kindest, happiest thing to do now?" Stands must be taken. If I am to respect myself I have to search myself for what I believe is right and take a stand on what I find. Otherwise I have not gathered together what I have been given; I have not embraced what I have learned; I lack my own conviction.

I visited an alternative school today. After classes one of the instructors and I took a station wagon full of eight- to thirteen-year-old boys out to a construction site. Lining the foundation excavation were mounds of dirt ranging in height from ten to thirty feet. The instructor had come to pick up a backhoe, and while he worked on starting it, I watched the boys play on the mounds. They started jumping off the lower ones, then moved up in height. Three of the boys progressed very quickly, but I was impressed with the seriousness of one of the boys who did not. Even though it had already been tried by the others, he began working on overcoming his fear of jumping off one of the smaller hills. I could see the struggle in his face. The most he could expect would be a victory over himself, and that is what he accomplished. Then he moved on to the next hill, seemingly unmindful of the jeers from the other boys.

Today I found myself complaining to Gayle about chores I had to do for an incapacitated friend. Poor me. Yet I noticed that I was also a little pleased about the burden. There are a surprising number of inconveniences and difficulties that take on an aura of importance. Every week a man has a new story about how badly he's been treated by his supervisor. A couple makes the rounds announcing that they are getting divorced. A woman repeatedly describes the time she was so sick she almost died. These disclosures are usually reacted to as if they are accomplishments. But none of these events are necessarily meaningful. They may break the status quo and get our attention, but they are still only what we make of them. Today I tried to benefit from a friend's hardship.

It's obvious that many of the problems I have are the result of how things were when I was growing up. So here I am spending the rest of my life suffering for personality traits I never asked for. Where is the justice in that? There isn't any. But that begs the question. My childhood is over, so exactly when will I be old enough to take responsibility for what I am?

Maybe we are deluding ourselves with all our
theories of growth and techniques of improvement.
Maybe the truth is that progress is beyond our
comprehension, but since that fact is unbearable, we
busy ourselves with concepts. We read articles, listen
to authorities, have insightful discussions, yet I
wonder if we have any real idea where we are
headed. Maybe we can't alter the path of our lives. If
we were allowed to walk in the direction we seek to
walk, maybe it would be a disaster. When I look at
myself at thirteen, or twenty, or even at forty, I see
that I had no grasp of the principal changes that
were occurring in my life. What I believed— the
books I read, the concepts I spouted— were mostly
beside the point. Now I think that I have at least a
partial perception of the overall pattern of my life. I
believe it is possible for me to act in a way that will
positively affect, if not the outcome, then the
character, of my life. But I also believed that then.

I used to act as if I were racing after some magical thought. No new system could be left unbelieved. I swallowed whole every supposition fed to me. Anything was acceptable as long as it was unprovable. It was as if one day I might think the thought that would break me out. They were up there listening, and if I thought the right thought they would invite me up. Then I would sigh and say, "Wasn't that an experience!" They would smile knowingly, and I would be one of them. If only words and thoughts were that powerful. Then I would not have to do all this work in the trenches of relationship.

If I have to think of something in order to act
differently, no real change has yet taken place.

A new idea has energy, but like a new battery in an old five-battery flashlight, its power is temporary. It is natural for me to return to comfortable patterns and once again to think thoughts that are familiar. To be constantly reminding myself to change requires an effort that can't be sustained. Nor should it be. The longer I coerce myself to follow a concept that no longer inspires me, the more I must trample my own love and intuition. Nothing is gained by pushing a good idea beyond its season. An idea can inspire me, but it is not inspiration. A change within my core comes very slowly. I will be fortunate if I learn, really learn, one or two lessons in my life. The implication, of course, is that there is more to come.

Honest individuals do not find themselves in agreement with every enumerated belief held by the group of which they are members. If I don't take what I read or what I am told and weigh it against my own experience, of what value am I to myself?

As our experience teaches us the reliability of our own point of view, we begin to entertain the dangerous suspicion that all those talking heads out there may not know what they're talking about. The source is not the thing. One friend is not love. One person's teaching is not salvation. Yet salvation begins with loving one person.

Time does not separate us from the future and the
past in absolute, either-or terms. The present, past,
and future are more like lanes of traffic moving side
by side. Now we are in a present lane, but
occasionally we slip into a lane within the future, as I
did in yesterday's tennis match when I saw an exact
picture of the upcoming point. The experience was
not unnatural. I sensed that something like it had
happened many times. I suspect it does with
everyone. Just as does *déjà vu*. So the future is not only
imminent, it is here; it can be dealt with. And the
past is also within reach; it can still be healed.

My circumstances, my fortune good or bad, do not reflect the movement of my life. God does not reward the right beliefs with money. If I move toward love, I receive and experience more love, not more good fortune. The feeling is, I am becoming more like myself. That implies either a potential wholeness or a concurrent wholeness. If in some sense I am already what I am changing into, then possibly I can draw more fully upon that existing state.

When at last I think I have changed, I notice that the
change feels familiar, that it is not new, that I can
recall other times I have felt or acted this way, at
least in part. Then, inevitably, the change begins to
dissipate. But in not quite the same way as before. It
stays longer this time around, or it leaves more of
itself behind. Change is the return of something
once known, something that will not be abandoned.
I look down the line of my life and I see it surfacing
again and again. I recognize it. I am that thing. I am
being put back together.

This special relationship I have presumed. I walk along talking to "him"—that seems a little ridiculous now. But not so ridiculous as "it," God the It. To think of all the empathy, caring, pathos, all the love in the universe caged inside these puny skulls seems absurd, as if love were a mutation—we have it, the ants don't. The bloodless laws of physics nurturing a seed of love into flower, an aberration on the edge of the universe, a few embers that long for fire; me, feeling love, insisting in my dementia that where there is a little there must be a lot—God the Lot. But I believe that. I do not believe we are freaks.

The talking does something. I pray to God, my
friend, and it changes me, if only for a moment. I feel
myself siding with what is good in me. I feel
cleansed, and I look around with more gentleness.
Relationships appear to re-form on a new basis: the
gentleness in me recognizing the gentleness in
others. I sense my own beauty and wholeness, and I
see a core of goodness in others. The world dances
for a moment. Now, if I can feel it, see it, act it, and
time and again it is handed back to me, then I should
know it exists. So why am I fighting to believe this?

I keep wanting to use the word *wholeness,* but is that in fact what all this holiness lacks? Maybe it's not complete. There is no falling-down-on-the-floor hilarity, no sex, no spit, no anger. It is soft and beautiful, and sooner or later I crave something more. The question is, Can one have both, both pain and caress, passion and peace, hubris and warmth? That is the conflict I have not yet answered. I still think there is something to be said for a fist in the stomach. I wouldn't want it as a way of life. I could never say, Now, I want the fist now. It would have to be unexpected, unplanned. When you've been without wounds you know it. As in a dreamless sleep, you yearn for at least one succubus, one grinning vampire in the night. So, what is my goal now? Both a knife and a healing touch? No wonder I'm fighting to believe in God—I still want God's opposite.

Several of Ann's friends confronted her a couple of weeks ago. They said, "Ann, why do you drink so much?" She answered, "Because I like to get drunk." One of them told me that those words essentially ended the conversation. They had all been there, done that, and they knew there are some things no one can teach you.

If there is no God, no all-embracing intelligence and love, if there are only a few pieces of brain scattered through the universe and everything else in this cold yawning vacuum is dead dust and an occasional quantum of light, then I am only talking to the better side of my own nature; I am appealing to my own instincts of love and courage. And there is something to be said for that. But I don't want to be deluded. If I am talking only to myself then I want to know that. Of course, both could be true, and the part of myself I am talking to is connected, joined, in fact, part of something bigger.

It's important not to overstate it, not to argue more than I know. The spiritual can't be caught in a handful of words. You have to just see it and accept it. That's the way it is. It's that way because it's that way.

No one ever gets it right. As long as there are humans, there will never be someone who will get it all right. My tendency is always to huddle over my little pile of bromides, to state things easily, and to make simple nodding movements with my head.

There we were today having another intense little discussion about spiritual reality. Isn't anything sacred to me? If it really means that much, how can I talk about it? Isn't there anything so precious that I simply would not smudge it with a single word?

Everything I write seems to be coming out dark. I have spent eight years trying to be honest and my unconscious has finally taken me seriously. No matter how good things get, my capacity to make myself unhappy is always equal to it.

Here I am taking this beetle outside and a mosquito bites me on my bald spot. When I was hairy and pubescent I would never have undertaken such an inglorious rescue. Now my patch of hard-won compassion is abused. My hair is coming out. At a reasonable rate. It's giving me plenty of time to adjust. Now if I had a hair transplant, would I suspend myself in time? Surgically remove wrinkles and replace hair, and we gain aesthetically, but do we lose something else of value? Is my body a lecture being delivered to me by the universe that I would be attempting to censor?

It is this never-ending, all-American, all-consuming war against aging that I don't want to get caught up in, this useless battle to check the advance of every wrinkle. It is an attempt, like so many others, to not be here. Dye the hair? Whiten the teeth? Freeze off the blemishes? As with money issues, the question isn't whether I should do it or not do it. Rather, it is which choice will allow me to think about my body less. Perhaps the decision is, Will I lean toward pettiness and myopia on one side, or grandeur and freedom on the other?

I observe, partly in horror, that my body is off on some course known only to itself. It never reached the promised plateau. The changes at midlife are as rapid as at puberty. I've been put on a roller coaster. I guess I can either stand up and yell to be let off, or sit back and enjoy it.

This parade of old schoolmates. I can see they have
been walking into a terrible wind. I look at them and
I know for certain I am going to die.

Stopped in my car, waiting to cross a line of traffic, I
used to think, "Maybe I can make it." Recently I've
been thinking, "Maybe I *can't* make it." I don't know
which question is better in life, but I do know which
is better for the other drivers.

When you're halfway there, you stop disbelieving in
there.

The energy and time I have wasted during my life thinking about my body, worrying about almost every part of it at one period or another: my chin is too long, my neck is not long enough, my nose should be more delicate, and on and on. Now age is handing me a new set of appearance changes to worry about. It occurred to me this morning that probably the irony in store for me is that it was never my body anyway; it was a rented house. Certainly it's true that as I get to know someone well I think of him or her less as a body. My attention is on something inside the heart.

"You have such lovely hair," I said. "Oh but it used to be thicker," she answered. "And it used to grow down to here." That is the way we kill ourselves. That is the way we die. All day we are waging these little wars of comparison against ourselves and others. The darkness accumulates in our minds like poison.

"Premature aging"—that phrase gives it away. Aging is OK, but not premature aging. If aging is OK, aging is OK. Time is recorded on our faces, in our muscles; we see its shadow moving across our childhood friends. What if we saw no passage of time? Then I suspect there would be many areas in which we wouldn't grow; our spirit would remain adolescent.

The body can't be forced to live the life of the mind.
Nor does the mind have to follow the lead of the
body. When I am sick I must withdraw my body, but
I can keep my mental arms around Gayle.

I think I would take better care of my body if I thought of it as a dog. I know what our German shepherd shouldn't eat and shouldn't sniff. I have little trouble saying no to her desire to sniff and eat dead birds, because I love her. If I truly loved my body, it would hear a lot more "no's."

What we don't know is whether the threescore and ten is about all the time we could profitably use anyway. Given the inescapable boundaries of my life—a male Caucasian, the only child of Virginia and Hugh, possessing all my limbs and certain governing childhood memories—could I really benefit from being that same person for, say, two hundred years? Maybe there's something to be said for just trusting the general order of things. Not trusting God to go around and fiddle with every detail, but trusting that we are watched over in about the same way that a loving parent watches over a sleeping child. How else can we explain the totally irrational feeling that most of us get sooner or later that everything is in God's hands and that we are loved?

They said it again. "She's burning the candle at both ends." "More fire to her," I said. "But Hugh, she's not going to last long at this rate." That shut me up. I certainly wouldn't want to be heard calling for early demise. However, the subject shouldn't have ended there. True, she may not last long, but is lasting long the most one can hope for? She's burning at both ends, but aren't we all? Our mind and muscle smolder even while we sit clucking at her wild thrashings. She at least feels something. What is the virtue in being just a piece of kindling, one curled shaving of self-righteousness? When it's all over, when nothing remains but to pull up the sheet, is that all they will have to say: "He outlived his friends by 7.4 years"?

They have a woman down at the morgue who can't be identified. She's been there for more than three weeks. I don't remember Santa Fe ever exerting itself in quite this way before. Both papers are on it. It seems to be on everyone's mind. The Glorieta Center has even made a public offer to bury her. I think we are all slightly horrified that anonymity can come so easily.

When you get knocked down, you lie there and you say, "It's pointless. None of this makes any difference." And because it is pointless, that truth comforts you and gives you time to heal. But once you have mended, the very futility that gave you rest now impels you to even greater effort. The impossibility of it all: the certain deterioration and death, the ponderous broom of history sweeping away all traces of individual lives, motivates you more than the hope of a thousand golden statues or trumpets or coins. It is because it will eventually mean nothing that you must do it.

Look at all these heroics. Here is my friend Mr.
Farrington, eighty-one years old, still saying all he
wants out of life is to write novels. His work has
diminished in both quality and volume. He hasn't
had a successful book in twenty years. But he isn't
lying. I know I will feel the same way. He wants to do
it, he knows he can still do it, and yet he is wrong.
He will never again equal what he did twenty years
ago. That, however, will not stop him. He's a
member of this species that strains off of two legs
just so it can keep its head as far as possible from the
ground, and which, even when it knows that the
very cells of the brain are shrinking, strives to go on,
to create, to achieve, to better itself just one more
time.

I have been working on a book for my friend for almost a year, and I have known all along that something is wrong. Now I see what it is. My motive has been good, the writing has been adequate, but the quality of the effort has not been equal. There was no power, no impelling urgency to my labor. Now that I have doubled my hours and am attempting something approximating a daily schedule, I feel more fully used, more integral to the project, and also more deserving of any good results. It is not relevant that even though my pace was indifferent, the outcome was acceptable, because there was a spiritual imbalance. A sense of justice and merit were missing in the work. We must strive to do all things impeccably, or else we betray our core.

There doesn't appear to be a way to give someone else what you know. Whenever I think I have succeeded in keeping someone from going through one more little hell, the long run proves me wrong. We each have to learn it all over again for ourselves. If we say we are all in God's hands, perhaps it is arrogant to believe we can improve on the job.

It wasn't until I was almost thirty-two that I began to believe in death. We were living in Berkeley, where I was starting my second year as an unpublished writer. It was about two in the morning and Gayle was asleep. As I lay in bed I was seized with a nearly absolute conviction that I wasn't going to live to see daylight. I got out of bed and went to the living room. I began to think of all that I had not done with my life, the friends I had neglected, things I had made important that were not important, and I started crying. I cried off and on for several hours, and when the sun finally rose I had begun writing. What I wrote later became the opening pages of my first published book. There had been no apparent reason for me to fear death; I wasn't sick, nor was I in any danger. I think, very simply, the time had come for me to take my dying seriously. We are nudged to grow whether we want to or not, and for me that is a comforting fact. It evidences at least one aspect of the workings of the universe that could be compared to human love. In being urged to look at my own mortality, I was in some way being cared for, because the result was that I gained respect for the common material of my life and began a more considerate use of the time I had left.

Now he says he wants to be a writer. But when I tell him about the groundwork, the years of going unpublished, the filing cabinet full of false starts and rejected manuscripts, his eyes drift and he asks about all the letters and phone calls and the royalties. He is thinking about the time when the preliminaries will be over. But the preliminaries are never over. If it's worth getting there then you never quite make it. He has the facility and the charm, he may even have talent, but he lacks a certain infatuation with toil. He hungers for the goal but not for the struggle. Writing doesn't differ from his other endeavors that never succeeded. The obsession has to be with the process, the act of putting one word down after another. No one sees you do that, and by the time most people get around to reading what you have written, you are preoccupied with the next project and find yourself a little annoyed with criticism or praise for something that to you is clearly over and done with. Effort is in the present; results are in the future. If we don't make a good effort, we don't have a good present.

My life will make a statement. When I am on my deathbed, I will look back and my actions will say, "If only he hadn't rushed," or they will say, "He loved his family," or they will say, "He traded his talent for money." When that moment comes, I hope I will have given myself the finest I was capable of. I hope that what I do will make a bed on which I can take my rest.

Can a life be looked at as one thing? Can I see my life whole and make it into something new, a work of grace? What I have to deal with is for the most part garbage. When I look at it in one sweep, it is not noble. I have done little more than get by. As a teenager and as a young man, there were moments when I yearned to transcend myself, but overall I see no theme. Like a wind-up toy dropped randomly on the Earth, I climb over one thing only so I can climb over the next. Who or what set me in this direction? Nothing did, nothing but chance. At least I can try to take my life into my own hands and finish well. A painting, a song, a poem can transform in the final seconds of composing. I once saw Maldarelli do it with a sculpture. As he hammered off the last few chips of alabaster, the bust started to live; it was dead and it came to life.

More is out there than is inside this body. I don't want to be afraid to believe. I want to long for something. I don't want to be afraid to stick my hand up and grope above the clouds. I want to throw myself on my doubts. One has to be devastated. Time and again one has to be torn apart by the facts.

Too late for what?

Every great life dares. Like a man or woman of extraordinary beauty, it is almost ugly. Each attempt approaches the grotesque in its reach.

I am old enough. I have been given the lessons. More
than needed. More than I have ever used. The time
has come for me to put an end to this busy stocking
of supplies. I don't require one thing beyond the
counsel of my own heart. Why should I keep filling
myself with new reminders and techniques—it's
nothing other than procrastination. I can trust
myself. I know what to do.

Now is the time to take possession of my life, to start the impossible, a journey to the limits of my aspirations, for the first time to step toward my loveliest dream. "If I had only known then what I know now"—but now I know enough to begin.

There was a time when love was in my spirit. It created a pure burning in my eyes, a flame taken from a star. I could see it pouring like oil onto the shoulders of my friends. Like light in the dust it was even in my dreams. But now my thoughts are the thoughts of dogs, and my struggles are the wars of insects. My feet are bloodied, but the direction is known.

The time comes when you know you are going to die— not from imminent danger; danger is an accident, and accidents pass. It is the realization of the very limits you have been given, of the years you have run through, and of just how much of it you have left. The experience is at first horrifying, but after the horror fades, you are left with a perspective by which you can judge the relative worth or pointlessness of the countless activities you are engaged in and that until then you had let pass unexamined. At this point you may become quite arbitrary in your refusal to do certain things that before were routine. Now you know it is a question of time, and it is your time, not theirs, you are being asked to give up. But reality eventually forces you to take a second look, and what you see begins to dissolve your selfishness. You see that you are not alone, that your time will not be spent alone, that your life is in fact many lives, and that no matter how determined you are to make it so, your happiness cannot be solitary. What you see is that there is something else as important to you as your own life.

This evening I happened to look out the window just as the sun was setting. Along with a feeling of awe there was the unmistakable sense of being carried away. For that one moment I knew it didn't make any difference that I was going to die. This small life of mine was not important. I belonged to that beauty, and everything was as it should be.

ABOUT THE AUTHOR

Hugh Prather is the author of fifteen books, including the bestselling *Notes to Myself, Spiritual Notes to Myself, A Book for Couples, Spiritual Parenting, The Little Book of Letting Go,* and *I Will Never Leave You.* He has more than thirty years of experience counseling couples, families in crisis, battered women and their abusers, and grieving parents who have lost children. For many years a resident minister at St. Francis in the Foothills United Methodist Church, Prather now lives in Tucson, Arizona, with his wife and co-author Gayle. There he does a daily radio program for wisdommedia.com and Serius Satellite Radio. He and Gayle have three boys and far too many pets.

TO OUR READERS

CONARI PRESS publishes books on topics
ranging from spirituality, personal growth, and
relationships to women's issues, parenting, and
social issues. Our mission is to publish quality books
that will make a difference in people's lives—how
we feel about ourselves and how we relate to one
another.

We value integrity, compassion, and receptivity,
both in the books we publish and in the way we do
business. As a member of the community, we donate
our damaged books to nonprofit organizations,
dedicate a portion of our proceeds from certain books
to charitable causes, and continually look for new
ways to use natural resources as wisely as possible.

Our readers are our most important resource,
and we value your input, suggestions, and ideas
about what you would like to see published. Please
feel free to contact us, to request our latest book
catalog, or to be added to our mailing list.

2550 Ninth Street, Suite 101
Berkeley, California 94710-2551
800-685-9595 • 510-649-7175 • fax: 510-649-7190
conari@conari.com • www.conari.com